Peter Søren

Bobbin Lace
for the Dining Table

Akacia

The publishing company and the author wish to thank Royal Copenhagen for the opportunity to photograph the laces with the royal dinnerware in their shop on Amager Square in Copenhagen.

Bobbin Lace for the Dining Table
© Peter Sørensen and Akacia Publication, Tommerup, Denmark 2009
Photography: P.E. Nikolajsen
Editor and Layout: I. L. Nikolajsen

Printers: Inprint, Riga 2009

ISBN: 978-87-7847-112-3

Introduction

Teaching gives me a great deal of joy and many challenges.
I have been teaching bobbin lace since 1991 and throughout the years I have made lots of designs for my students.

One day, one of my students wanted to make 12 doilies in Torchon Lace – but she did not want to repeat the same doily twelve times.

Therefore, I designed 12 different borders and mounted them on fabric.
The laces are divided into 3 groups: Mussel border No 1-4, Heart border No 1-4 and Fan border No 1-4.

This way the laces can be used for many different things such as, doilies, table runners, handkerchiefs and borders on christening gowns and wedding dresses.

Encouraged by my students the patterns for the 12 borders are collected in this book.

Everyone with knowledge of bobbin lace making can work these borders – have a go, and enjoy yourself.

Peter Sørensen
Agersted, August 2009

About the laces

The doilies measure 18 x 18 centimetres, but the number of bobbins range from 22 to 28 pairs.

All the working diagrams are shown in colours.

The twists shown at the beginning of the diagrams apply to the entire piece.

All the prickings are shown at full size for Linen 35/2 from Bockens.
If you want to make the laces in thicker or finer yarn, enlarge or reduce the pricking until the distance between 2 dots across is suitable for the chosen yarn – see the table below.

As gimp threads, use 3 threads of the same yarn as the lace is worked with.
Wind the three threads on the same bobbin.

All the laces are ended with reef knots – see figure 7 on page 7. The threads are cut about 8 centimetres from the knot.
After washing the threads are cut close to the knots.

The laces are mounted on linen fabric with 10 threads per centimetre.
If you are using thread of a different thickness the fabric must be adjusted.

Manufacturer	Thread Size	Distance between 2 dots across
Bockens	60/2	4 mm
Bockens	35/2	6 mm
Bockens	28/2	7,1 mm
Bockens	16/2	8 mm

Mounting on linen fabric

Figure 1

Lay the lace on the mounting fabric and fasten it
with pins - as evenly as possible.
Pull out one thread (A) of the fabric, along the four
inner sides of the lace.
Remove the pins again.
Count 4 threads outwards and pull the next 3 to 4
threads (B) out of the fabric, along the four sides
of the work.
Fasten the lace on the fabric again and tack it in
position.
Work a hemstitch.

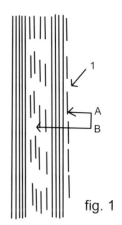

fig. 1

Figure 2 – Hemstitch

Step 1 (horizontal stitch): Sew twice around the
edge of the lace plus the four threads between A
and B.
Step 2 (vertical needle): In line A, take the needle
under 5 threads to the next stitch.
Step 3 (oblique needle): Take the needle back to
the previous hole and into the area B.
Repeat these three steps.
After the sewing, turn over, pull the extra fabric
back and cut it near the stitching.

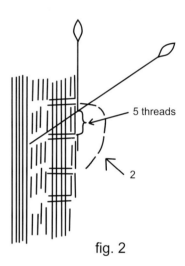

fig. 2

After-care

Lay the finished work in cold water for 24 hours
and then wash it gently in soapy water.
Let the work dry and press it gently.
Now, the ends of the lace threads are cut near the
reef knots.
Linen fabric shrinks 10% in the wash, but can be
pressed out again 5%.

Colour code

Green = Half stitch
Half stitch: Take the 2nd bobbin over the 3rd – take the 2nd bobbin over the 1st and the 4th bobbin over the 3rd.

Purple = Cloth Stitch
Cloth stitch: Take the 2nd bobbin over the 3rd – take the 2nd bobbin over the first and the 4th bobbin over the 3rd – take the 2nd bobbin over the 3rd.

Red: Whole stitch
Whole stitch: *Take the 2nd bobbin over the 3rd – take the 2nd bobbin over the 1st and the 4th bobbin over the 3rd*. Repeat from * to *.

Black = Twist, gimp pair, pin

  Black Square = Rose ground

Starting with a half stitch – half stitch before and after the pin

To start with a half stitch, hang two pairs on the top pin, twist (= take the 2nd bobbin over the 1st and the 4th bobbin over the 3rd) and make a half stitch – see figure 1.
Remove the pin and replace it in the same hole after the half stitch – see figure 2.
Make one more half stitch.

fig. 1

fig. 2

Starting with whole stitch – 3 pairs on the pin

The number 3 at the start in whole stitch indicates 3 pairs at the same pin. The work proceeds with 2 pairs outside the pin and one pair inside the pin – see figure 3.

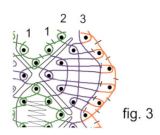

fig. 3

Small spider – in cloth stitch*

Make a cloth stitch with pair No 1 on the left side through pair No 3 and 4 on the right side – and pair No 2 through pair No 3 and No 4*.
Place a pin between the pairs, pull the threads together and repeat from * to * – see figure 4.

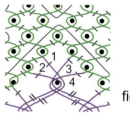

fig. 4

Fan – with pin inside 2 pairs

Whole stitch at the outer edge, place a pin inside 2 pairs.
The pair on left works cloth stitch in the fan – see figure 5.

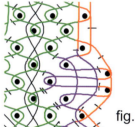

fig. 5

Tally

Start with 2 twists on both pairs.
Weave 8 to 10 times with the 2nd pair on the left (= the working thread) and end with 2 twists on both pairs – see figure 6.

fig. 6

Reef knot – with an extra twist

Put the right thread around the left thread and pull the threads to the pin.
Then put the threads around each other twice and pull them together – see figure 7.

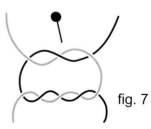

fig. 7

Mussel border No 1

28 pairs linen 35/2
3 gimp bobbins

Start as shown on the working diagram.

Foot side: Whole stitch – pin inside 2 pairs.
The ground: Half stitch with an extra twist.
The rectangles: Cloth stitch
The tallies are surrounded by: Half stitch with an extra twist.
The mussel: Cloth stitch with whole stitch at the outer edge
– pin inside 2 pairs (foot side).

Mussel border No 1

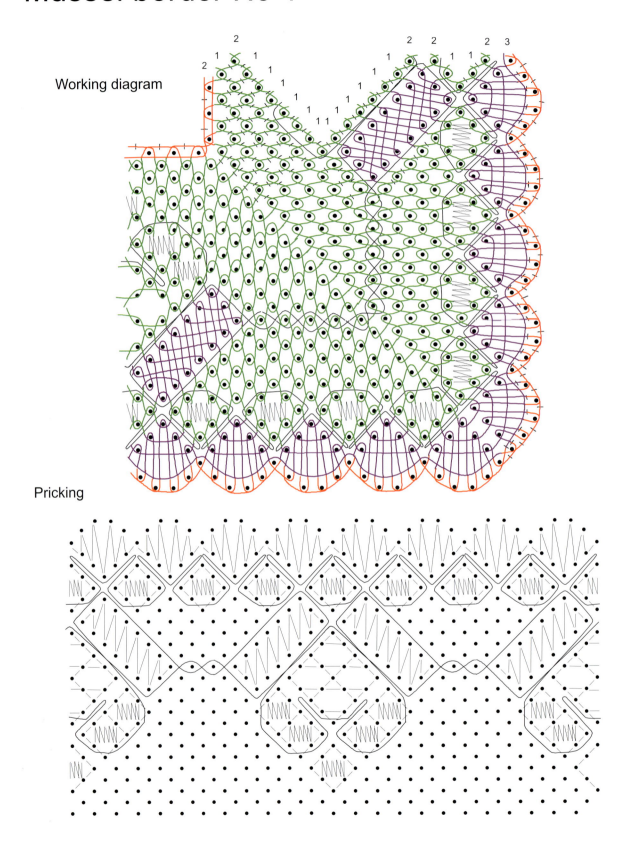

Working diagram

Pricking

Mussel border No 1

Pricking

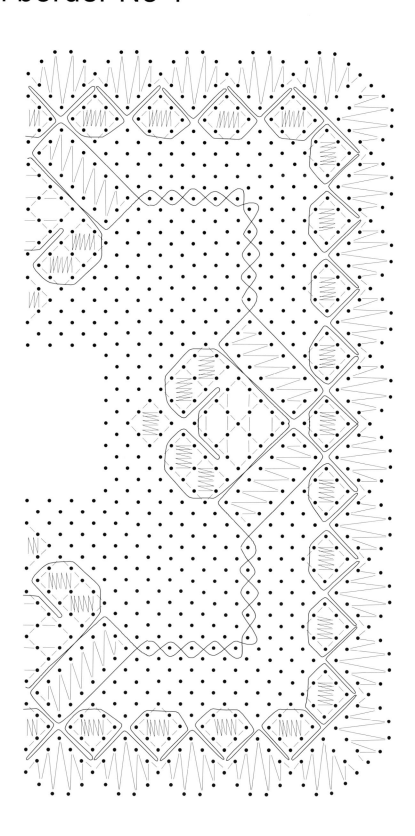

Mussel border No 2

26 pairs linen 35/2
3 gimp bobbins

Start as shown on the working diagram.

Foot side: Whole stitch – pin inside 2 pairs.
The ground: Half stitch with an extra twist.
Rose ground: Half stitch.
The mussel: Cloth stitch with whole stitch at the outer edge
– pin inside 2 pairs (foot side).

Mussel border No 2

Working diagram

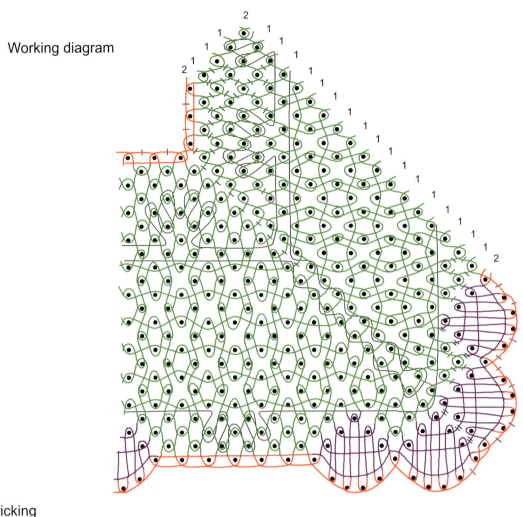

Pricking

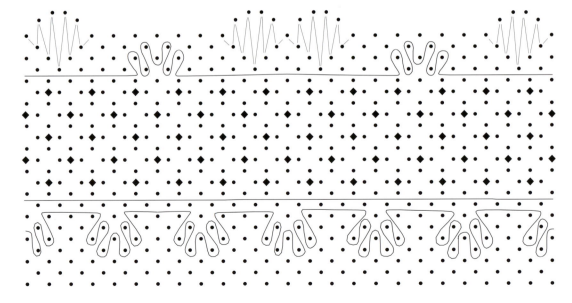

Mussel border No 2

Pricking

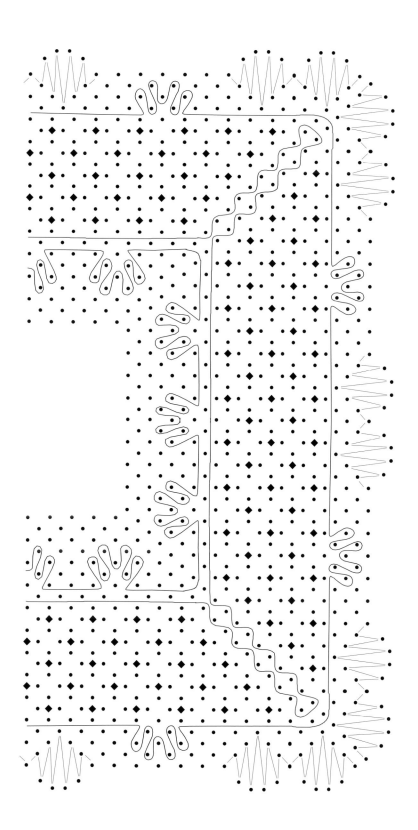

Mussel border No 3

26 pairs linen 35/2
2 gimp bobbins

Start as shown on the working diagram.

Foot side: Whole stitch – pin inside 2 pairs.
The ground: Half stitch with an extra twist.
Rose ground: Half stitch.
Bias ground: Half stitch and cloth stitch.
The mussel: Cloth stitch with whole stitch at the outer edge
– pin inside 2 pairs (foot side).

Mussel border No 3

Working diagram

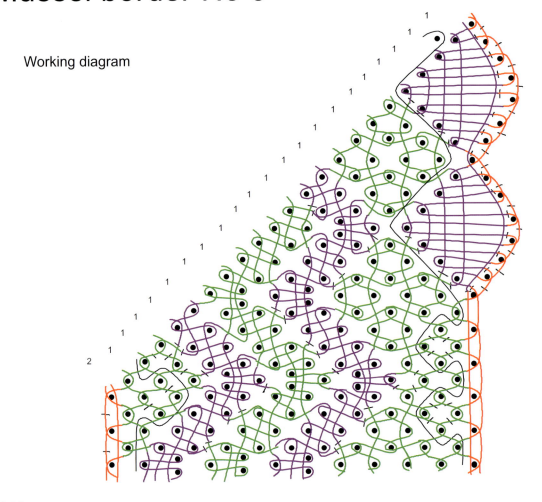

Pricking

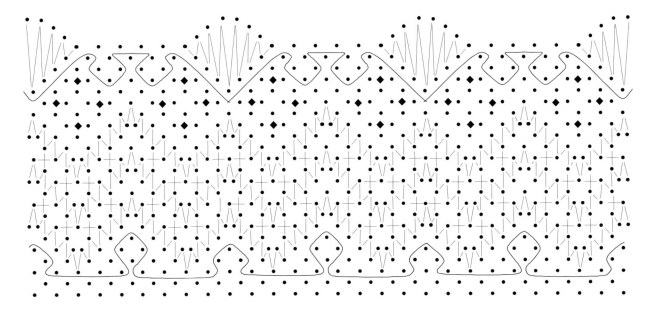

Mussel border No 3

Pricking

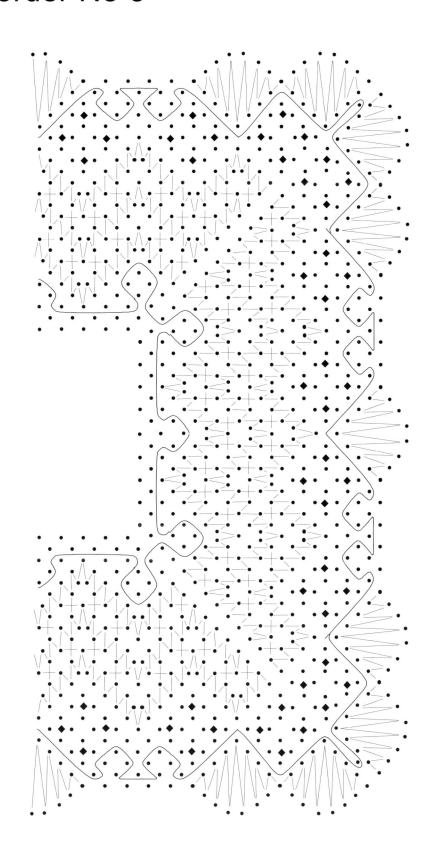

Mussel border No 4

26 pairs linen 35/2
2 gimp bobbins

Start as shown on the working diagram.

Foot side: Whole stitch – pin inside 2 pairs.
The ground: Half stitch with an extra twist.
Small spiders: Cloth stitch.
Triangular ground: Cloth stitch.
The squares outside the gimp: Cloth stitch
The mussel: Cloth stitch with whole stitch at the outer edge
– pin inside 2 pairs (foot side).

Mussel border No 4

Working diagram

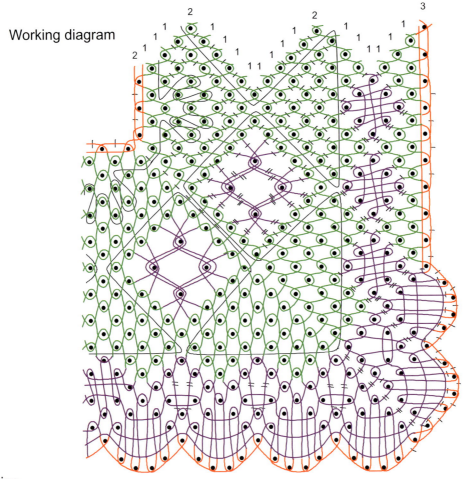

Pricking

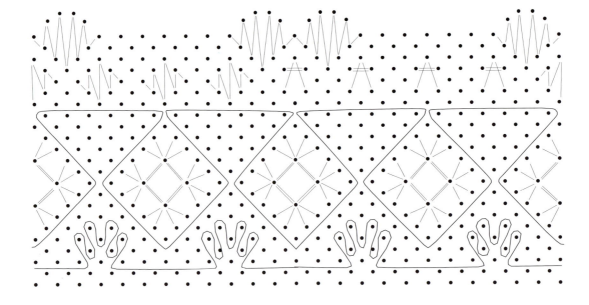

Mussel border No 4

Pricking

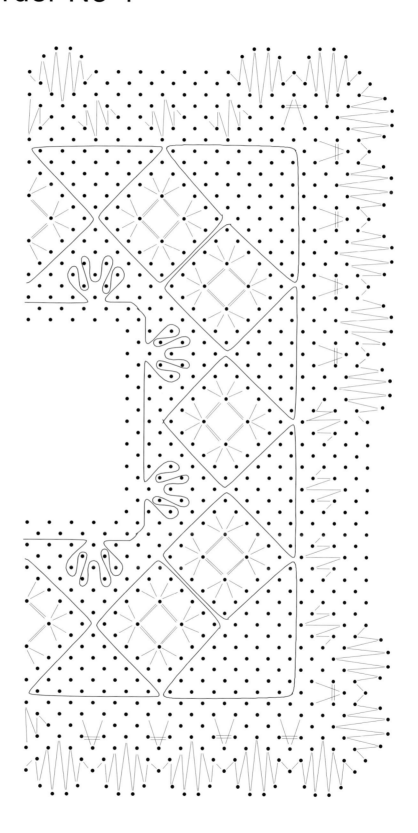

Heart border No 1

26 pairs linen 35/2
3 gimp bobbins

Start as shown on the working diagram.

Foot side: Whole stitch – pin inside 2 pairs.
The ground: Half stitch with an extra twist.
The inner Bias ground: Half stitch.
The outer Bias ground: Cloth stitch.
Triangular ground: Cloth stitch.
The tallies are surrounded by: Half stitch with an extra twist.
The heart: Cloth stitch with whole stitch at the outer edge – pin inside 2 pairs (foot side).

Heart border No 1

Working diagram

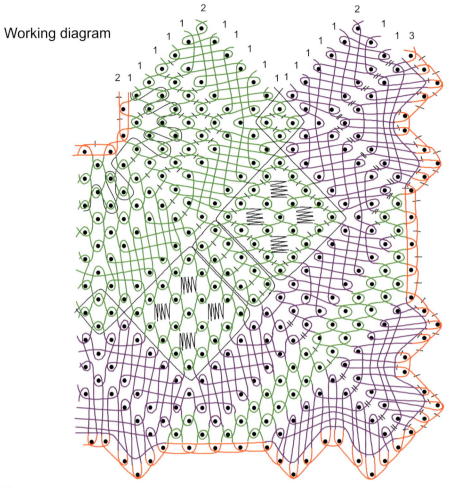

Pricking

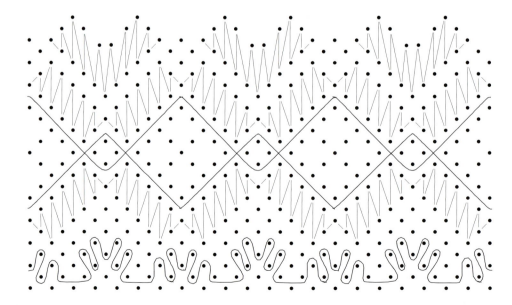

Heart border No 1

Pricking

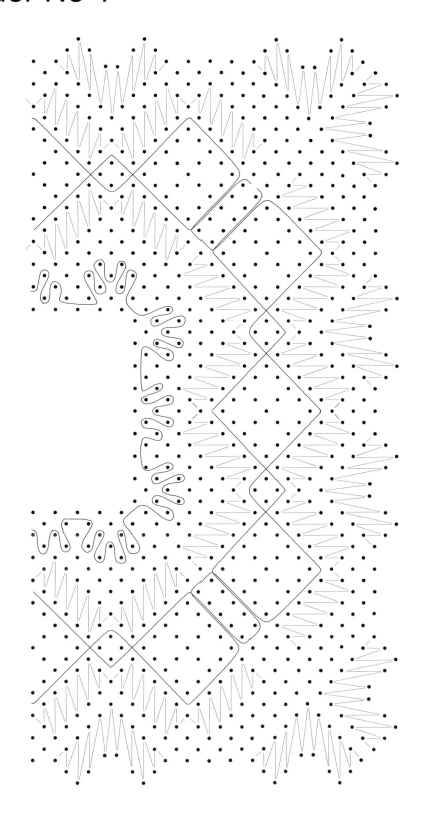

Heart border No 2

26 pairs linen 35/2
1 gimp bobbin

Start as shown on the working diagram.

Foot side: Whole stitch – pin inside 2 pairs.
The ground: Half stitch with an extra twist.
Small Bias ground: Cloth stitch.
Bias ground: Cloth stitch.
Triangular ground: Cloth stitch.
Rose ground: Half stitch.
The heart: Cloth stitch with whole stitch at the outer edge – pin inside 2 pairs (foot side).

Heart border No 2

Working diagram

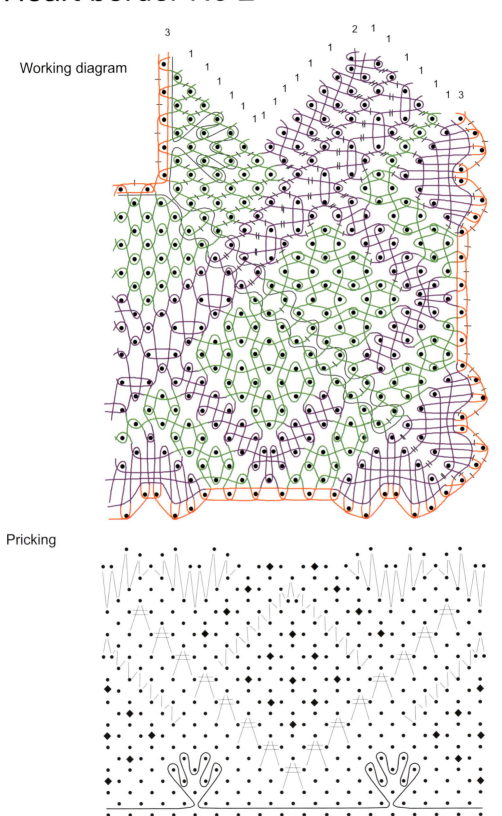

Pricking

Heart border No 2

Pricking

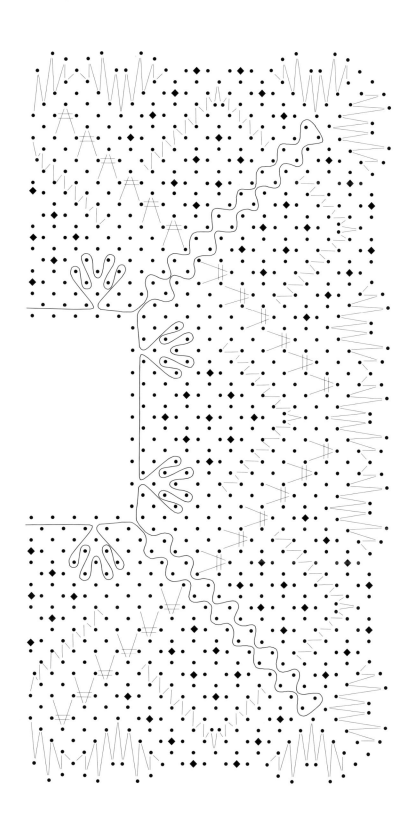

Heart border No 3

24 pairs linen 35/2
2 gimp pairs

Start as shown on the working diagram.

Foot side: Whole stitch – pin inside 2 pairs.
The ground: Half stitch with an extra twist.
Triangular ground: Cloth stitch.
The heart: Cloth stitch with whole stitch at the outer edge
– pin inside 2 pairs (foot side).

Heart border No 3

Working diagram

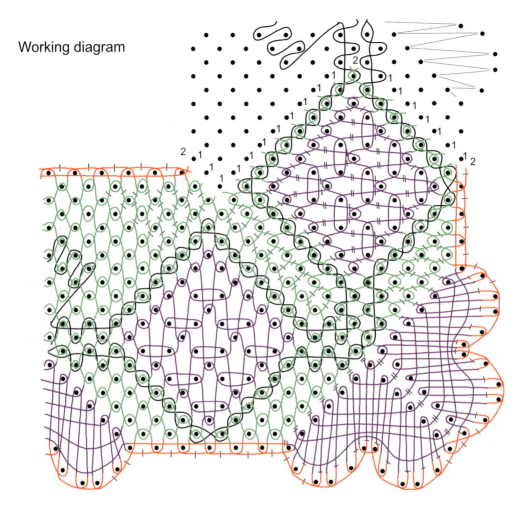

Pricking

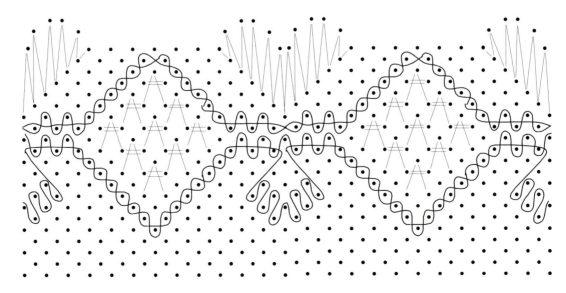

Heart border No 3

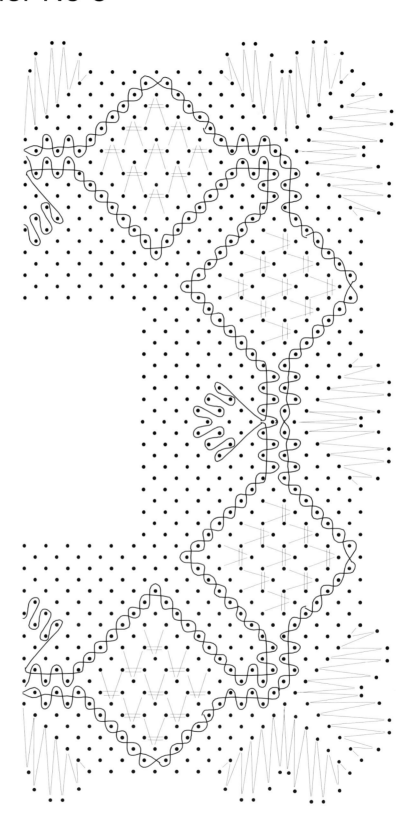

Heart border No 4

28 pairs linen 35/2
2 gimp pairs

Start as shown on the working diagram.

Foot side: Whole stitch – pin inside 2 pairs.
The ground: Half stitch with an extra twist.
The tallies are surrounded by: Half stitch with an extra twist.
Bias ground: Half stitch.
The heart: Cloth stitch with whole stitch at the outer edge
– pin inside 2 pairs (foot side).

Heart border No 4

Working diagram

Pricking

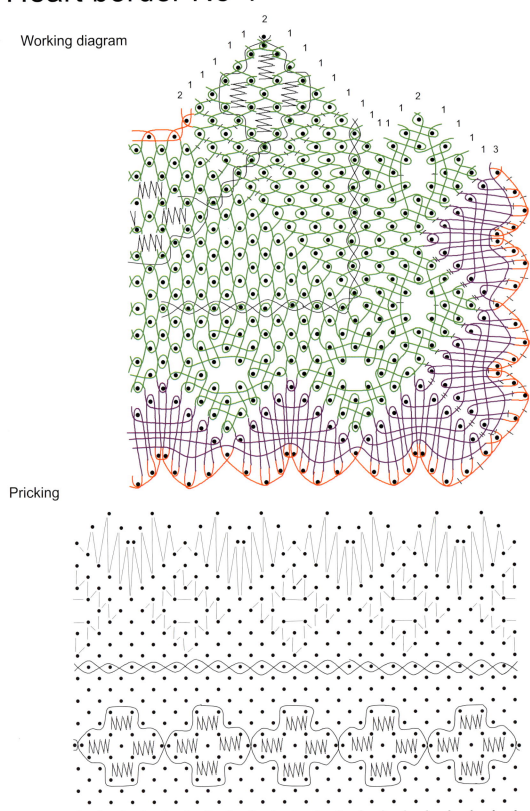

Heart border No 4

Pricking

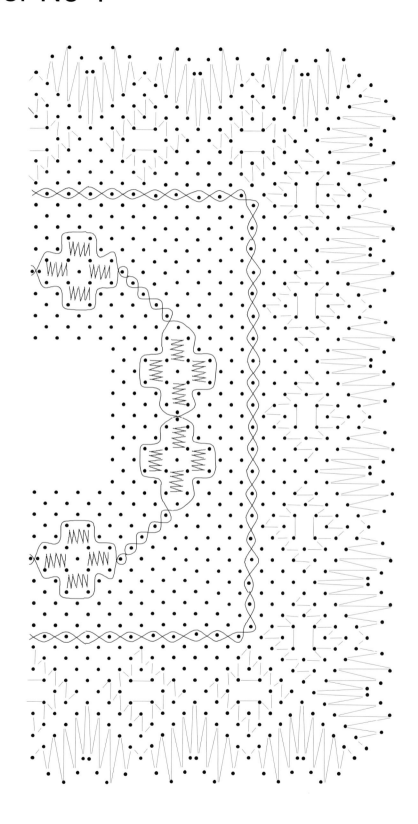

Fan border No 1

24 pairs linen 35/2
2 gimp bobbins

Start as shown on the working diagram.

Foot side: Whole stitch – pin inside 2 pairs.
The ground: Half stitch with an extra twist.
The tallies are surrounded by: Half stitch with an extra twist.
Bias ground: Half stitch.
Straight outer edge: Whole stitch – pin inside 2 pairs.
The fan: Cloth stitch with whole stitch at the outer edge – pin inside 2 pairs (foot side).

Fan border No 1

Working diagram

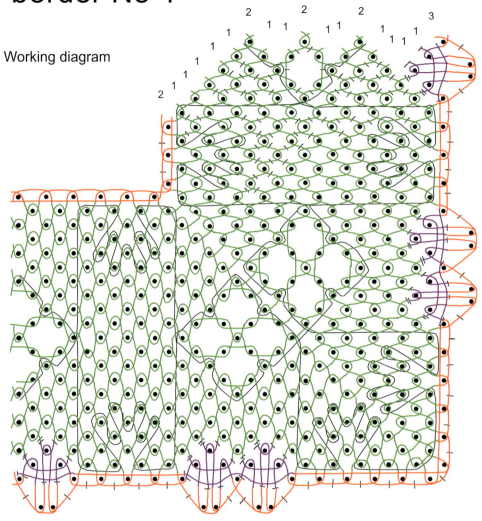

Pricking

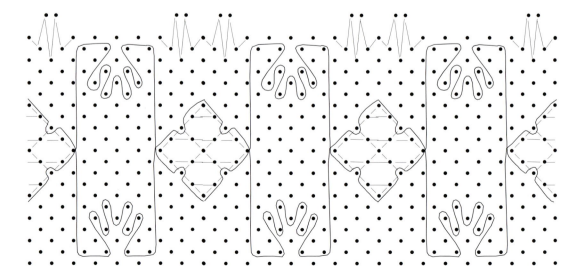

Fan border No 1

Pricking

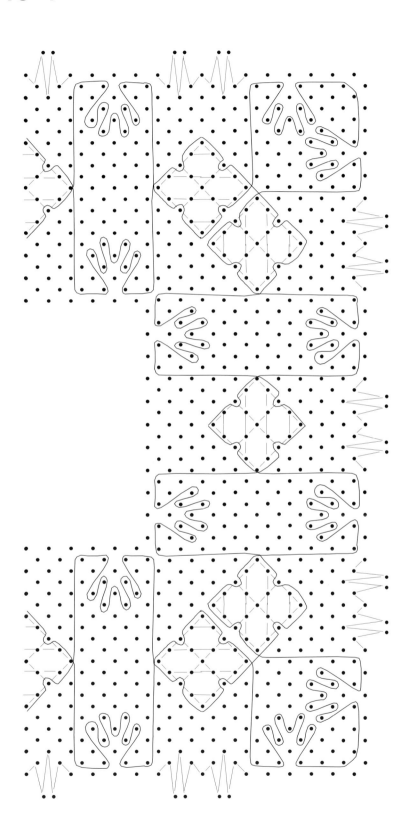

Fan border No 2

22 pairs linen 35/2
2 gimp pairs

Start as shown on the working diagram.

Foot side: Whole stitch – pin inside 2 pairs.
The ground: Half stitch with an extra twist.
Brabant ground: Half stitch with an extra twist.
Foot side: Whole stitch – pin inside 2 pairs.
The fan: Cloth stitch with whole stitch at the outer edge – pin inside 2 pairs (foot side).

Fan border No 2

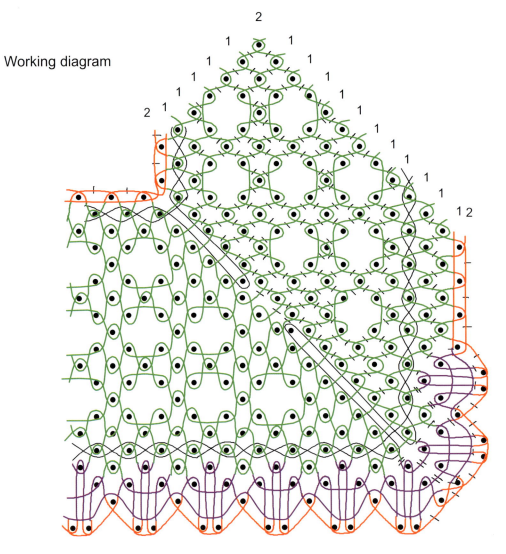

Pricking

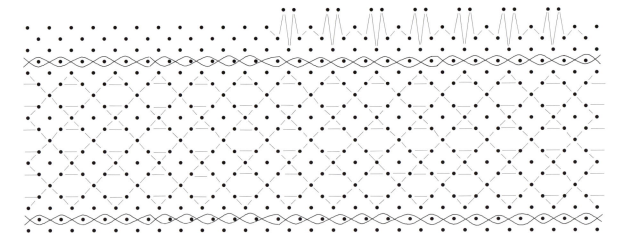

Fan border No 2

Pricking

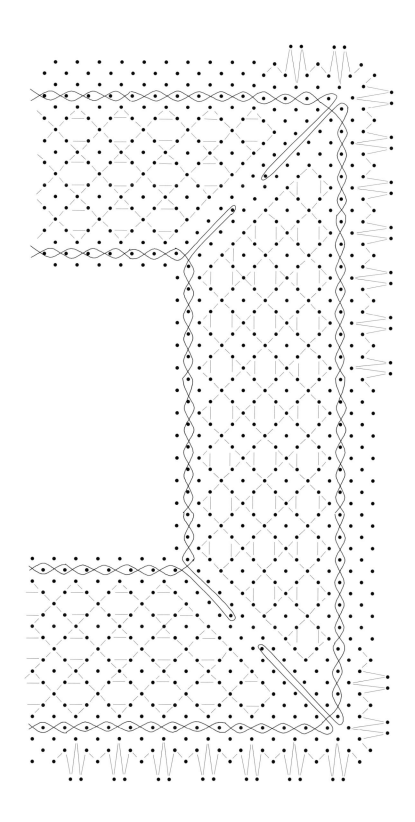

Fan border No 3

24 pairs linen 35/2
2 gimp bobbins

Start as shown on the working diagram.

Foot side: Whole stitch – pin inside 2 pairs.
The ground: Half stitch with an extra twist.
The tallies are surrounded by: Half stitch with an extra twist.
The fan: Cloth stitch with whole stitch at the outer edge – pin inside 2 pairs (foot side).

Fan border No 3

Working diagram

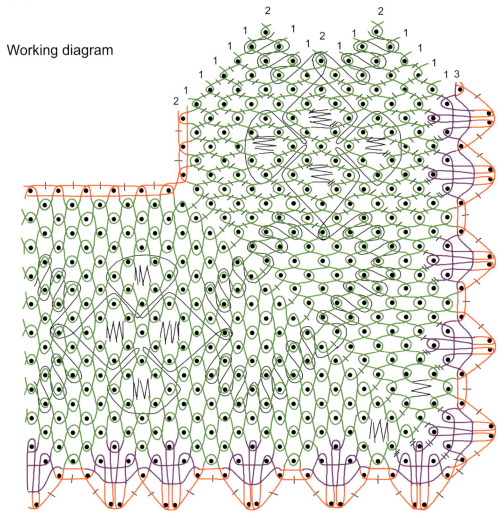

Pricking

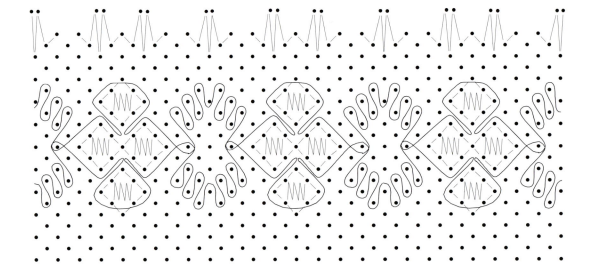

Fan border No 3

Pricking

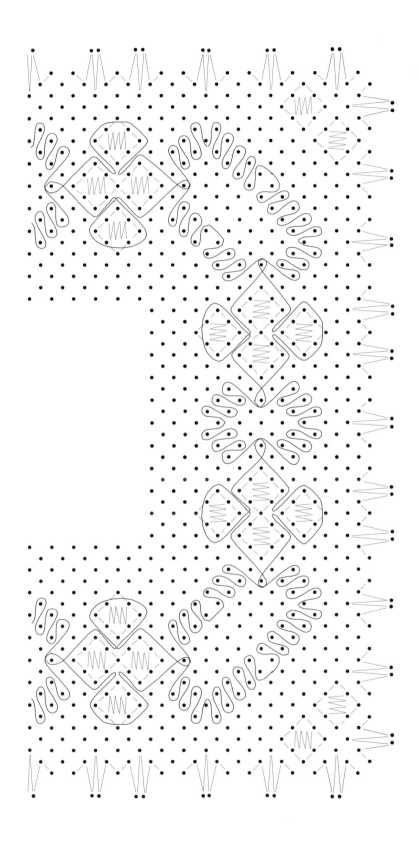

Fan border No 4

25 pairs linen 35/2
2 gimp bobbins

Start as shown on the working diagram.

Foot side: Whole stitch – pin inside 2 pairs.
The ground: Half stitch with an extra twist.
The tallies are surrounded by: Half stitch
Straight outer edge: Whole stitch – pin inside 2 pairs.
The fan: Cloth stitch with whole stitch at the outer edge – pin inside 2 pairs (foot side).

Fan border No 4

Working diagram

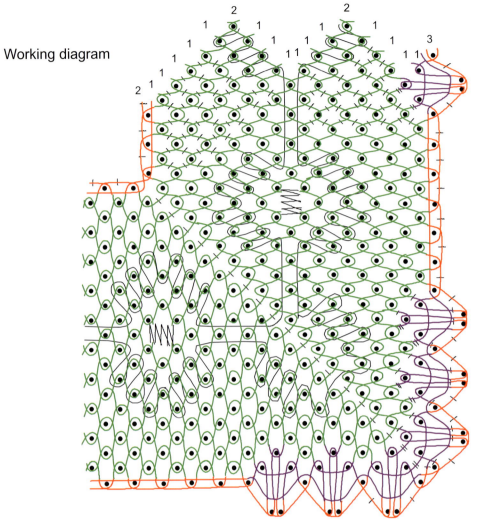

Pricking

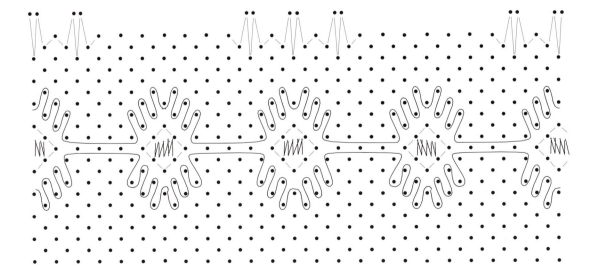

Fan border No 4

Pricking

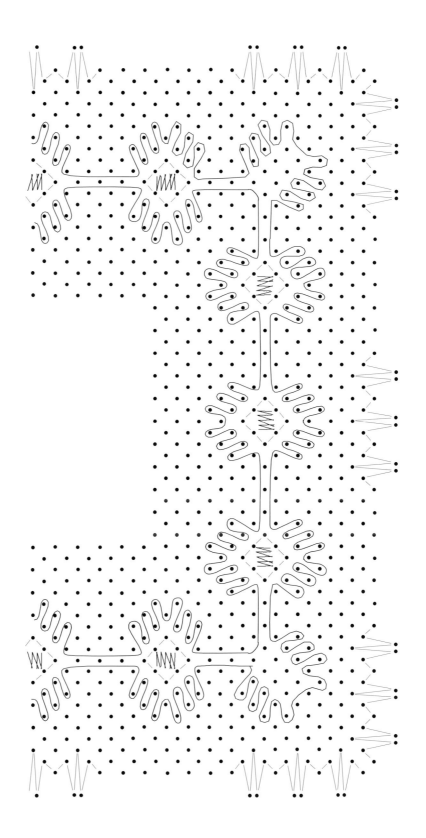